LEARN TO KNIT

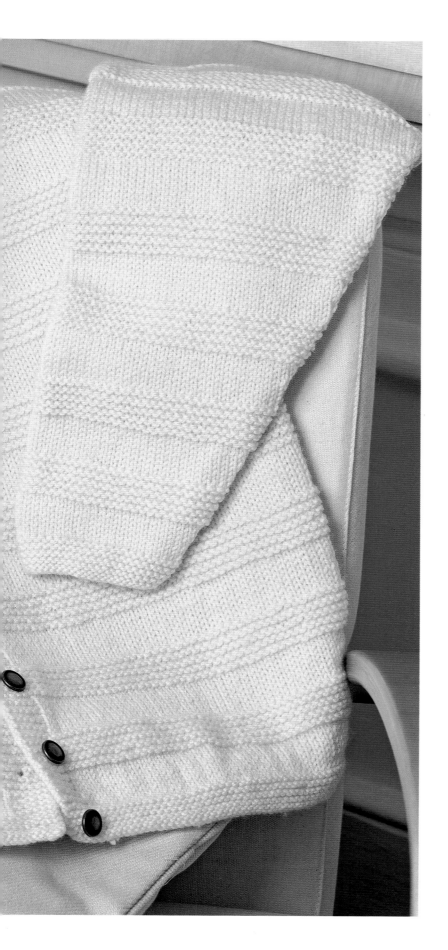

LEARN TO KNIT

PENNY HILL

CRE▲TIVE
ARTS & CRAFTS™

An imprint of CREATIVE HOMEOWNER, Upper Saddle River, NJ

First published in the United States and Canada in 2004 by

CRE▲TIVE
ARTS & CRAFTS™

An imprint of Creative Homeowner®
Upper Saddle River, NJ
Creative Homeowner® is a registered trademark of Federal Marketing Corp.

Current printing (last digit) 10 9 8 7 6 5 4 3 2 1
Library of Congress card number: 2003112173
ISBN: 1-58011-175-0

Senior Editor: Clare Sayer
Production: Hazel Kirkman
Design: Frances de Rees
Photographer: Shona Wood
Editorial Direction: Rosemary Wilkinson

Reproduction by Pica Digital PTE Ltd, Singapore
Printed and bound by Times Offset (M) Sdn. Bhd., Malaysia

CREATIVE HOMEOWNER
A division of Federal Marketing Corp.
24 Park Way
Upper Saddle River, NJ 07458
www.creativehomeowner.com

CONTENTS

INTRODUCTION

Knitting can be a perfect antidote to today's hectic, stress-filled life. It is calming and rewarding, and can even become habit-forming.

If you've never knit before, it's not too late to learn. Whether you shop in chain stores or in exclusive yarn boutiques, there is a large selection of yarn, from classic worsteds in a rainbow of colors to earthy textures. You'll find lots of inspiration. Specialty shops always have sales staff who can help to make a choice.

It's easy to teach yourself to knit with a little practice and some patience. Following the techniques shown in this book, you'll become an expert in no time. You can knit by yourself in front of the fire or with friends. The latter is a great opportunity to swap patterns and exchange ideas about how to use knitting to create clothes and accessories for the home.

Let's revive knitting as a skill that is passed from generation to generation. Pass on the skill to your sons and daughters and keep the art alive.

Penny Hill.

Basic Information

Yarn comes in a variety of thicknesses and textures and there are needles and gadgets galore. The following information will help you decide what you will need.

YARNS

Yarn is divided into two categories, natural and synthetic. Natural yarn is generally more expensive, but can be more pleasant to wear and easier to handle when knitting. Synthetic yarn is more economical and stronger.

Natural yarns

Wool is easily available, long lasting, and very warm. It is shorn from sheep, which are bred for their fleeces. Merino sheep have the most abundant and highest quality yarn.

Mohair yarn comes from goats that originated in Turkey. The long brushed fibers are extremely thick and warm.

Angora is an expensive, soft, and warm fiber that comes from the short-haired albino rabbit of the same name.

Cashmere is the most expensive and luxurious of yarns. Often spun with a high percentage of wool, it comes from a special breed of mountain goat.

Alpaca is a soft, high-quality fiber with a slight hairiness. It comes from a species of camel related to the llama.

Silk knitting yarns are heavy and expensive, but, when mixed with other fibers, it produces a strong, durable thread.

Cotton is a strong, non-allergenic, easy-to-wash yarn that has little elasticity.

Synthetic yarns

Man-made yarns have improved dramatically over the last few years — they are no longer lifeless with little elasticity. Combinations of synthetic (nylon, polyester, and acrylic) and natural fibers produce fashionable, strong, and lightweight yarns. The cost compares favorably with more expensive natural fibers.

Lurex is a shiny metallic yarn that comes in many colors or may be a single thread used as one of the plies when the yarn is spun.

Yarn thickness

Yarn is formed by twisting together a number of strands, or plies, of fiber: 3-ply, 4-ply, 8-ply. The most common thicknesses or weights are fingering or fine, sport or medium, worsted, bulky, and extra bulky.

BELOW, from top to bottom: wool, mohair, angora, tweed effect yarn, silk, cotton, lurex mix.

Yarn texture

During the spinning process, fibers can be fused together at different rates. Textured yarns tend to be more difficult with which to knit.

Bouclé is produced by introducing one ply at a faster rate than the other two, so that it buckles up or loops.

Mohair, a brushed loop yarn, has a fluffy appearance.

Slub yarns have at least one ply that varies in thickness, producing an uneven look.

Tweed effects are formed by adding colored blips to longer fibers.

EQUIPMENT

While all that is really needed to produce a piece of knitted fabric is a pair of knitting needles and some yarn, you may find some of these basic essentials useful, as well.

Needles

Needles are made of plastic, wood, bamboo, steel, or alloy. Whichever type you choose, it should make no difference to the gauge or quality of your work. It is all a matter of personal choice.

Pairs of needles These range in size from 0 to 15 (US) and come in three lengths: 10 inches, 12 inches and 14 inches. Use the length that you find most comfortable for the number of stitches you are working with and the type of pattern you are knitting.

Circular needles are used for knitting tubular, seamless fabrics or for knitting flat rounds. They consist of two short needles joined by a length of plastic that varies in length. They can also be used as a pair of needles, working backwards and forwards, for patterns with a large number of stitches. Always store the needles in their original, labeled packet because they do not have their size stamped on them.

Double-pointed needles are available in sets of four or six. They are often used to knit neckbands. They can also be an alternative to circular needles when a pattern has a small number of stitches that may be too stretched out on a circular needle. Double- pointed needles are for knitting seamless socks, gloves, and berets.

Cable needles are short straight needles (or they may have a U-bend), available in 3 sizes. They are used for moving stitches from one

ABOVE, from top to bottom: bouclé, mohair, ribbon yarn, tweed.

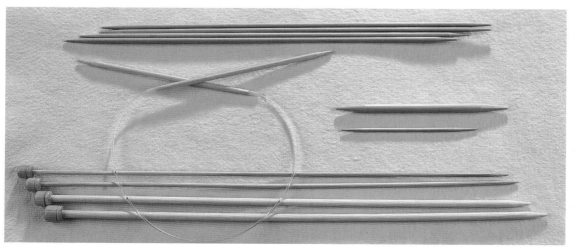

LEFT, clockwise from top: double-pointed needles, cable needles, pairs of needles, circular needles.

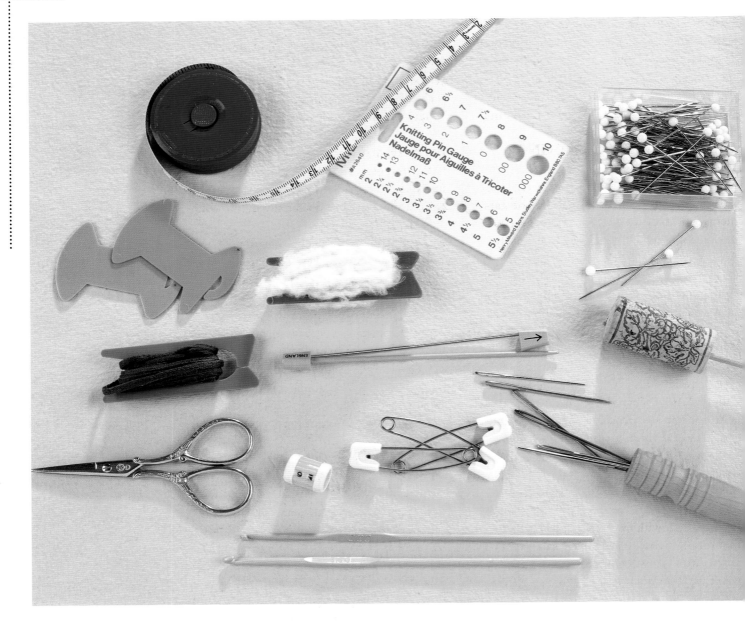

position to another when working cables. Use the size that corresponds to the type of yarn and main needles.

Other basics

Stitch-holders are useful for holding a small number of stitches until they are needed again.

Safety pins can be used instead of a stitch-holder for 4 or 5 stitches.

Tape measure Always use a plastic or plastic-coated tape measure that cannot stretch (and distort your measurements).

Scissors can be small but must be sharp because some yarns are very strong.

Pins can disappear in the knitting if they are too small, so choose long ones with colored glass or plastic heads.

Sewing needles with large eyes and blunt ends, such as tapestry needles, are used for sewing tasks because sharp needles can split the yarn and weaken it.

Needle gauges are useful for checking the sizes of circular and double-pointed needles, which do not have the size stamped on them.

Row counters are useful for keeping track of rows worked, particularly when increasing and decreasing.

Yarn bobbins can hold small amounts of yarn, wound from the main ball, when working color patterns.

ABOVE, top row, from left to right: tape measure, needle gauge, pins; middle row, from left to right: yarn bobbins, stitch holder, cork; bottom row, from left to right: scissors, row counter, crochet hooks, safety pins, needles.

Crochet hooks in small, medium and large sizes are useful for picking up dropped stitches and working edgings on finished garments. **Corks** can be used to put on the end of knitting needles to prevent stitches from falling off and to make them safer when not in use.

CLEANING AND STORING

It is best to clean hand-knitted garments lightly and often, but with great care. Hand-knits are not as resilient as ready-made garments, and they are more likely to stretch out of shape or shrink if not handled carefully. Always refer to the ball band of the yarn for cleaning or washing instructions. Unless the ball band specifically states that the yarn can be machine washed, it is safest to hand wash or dry clean.

Hand washing

Use a special mild solution for hand washing delicate fabrics. Completely dissolve the detergent in warm water, then add sufficient cold water to make the temperature lukewarm.

Immerse the garment in the suds and work quickly, using your hands to expel soapy water by gentle squeezing, never wringing.

Carefully lift the garment out of the water, supporting it with both hands. Rinse the garment well in clean water of the same temperature. After rinsing, squeeze out as much water as possible, but do not wring or twist.

Drying

Drying needs as much care as washing. Supporting the weight of the garment, transfer it to a clean colorfast towel and lay it flat. Roll up the towel loosely so that excess moisture is absorbed by the towel.

Lightly shake the garment to even out the stitches, lay it on a fresh dry towel, and gently reshape it back to its original form. Leave the garment to dry naturally until all the excess moisture has been absorbed by the towel.

You may machine-dry natural fibers on the short gentle cycle. Cotton should be dried in the machine because retained moisture may distort the garment.

Storage

Again, correct storage is as important as washing and drying. Never hang a knitted garment up, as the weight of the garment pulls it out of shape and the ends of the hanger can distort the shape of shoulders.

Folding a garment

1. Lay the garment on a flat surface with both sleeves fully extended.
2. Fold in one sleeve diagonally in line with the side of the garment.
3. Double the sleeve back on itself to form a straight edge with the side of the garment.
4. Repeat steps 2 and 3 for the other side.
5. Fold the garment in half and store.

If the garment is to be stored for a long time, interleave tissue paper in the folds and place the garment in a plastic bag (not tightly sealed) with lots of holes in it before storing.

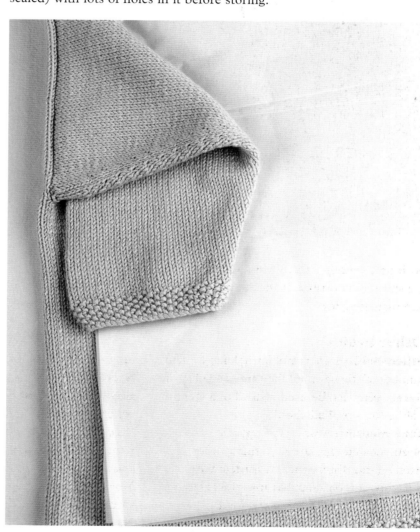

Get Ready to Begin

Before casting on, practice holding the needles and yarn. You have to master this in order to properly control the gauge of the fabric. There are several ways of casting on and knitting, including Continental methods. Use whichever feels most comfortable for you.

HOLDING THE YARN

1. Holding the yarn in the left hand, pass it under and around the little finger of the right hand, then take it over the third finger, under the second finger and over the index finger. The index finger is used to wind the yarn around the tip of the needle. The yarn around the little finger controls the tension of the yarn.

1

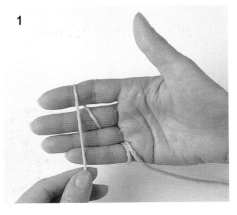

HOLDING THE NEEDLES

1. Hold the right needle in the same position as you would hold a pencil. When casting on and for the first few rows, the knitting passes easily between the thumb and index finger. As the knitting grows larger, place the thumb underneath the knitting, holding the needle from below.

1

Hold the left needle lightly over the top, using the thumb and index finger to control the tip of the needle.

CASTING ON — CABLE METHOD

This method of casting on gives a neat firm edge with a cable appearance.

1. Leaving enough yarn for sewing up the seam, make a slip knot and place it on the left-hand needle.

1

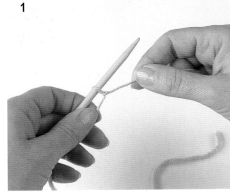

2. Holding the yarn at the back of the needles, insert the tip of the right-hand needle into the slip knot, and pass the yarn over the tip of the right-hand needle.

2

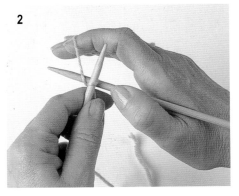

3. Draw the right-hand needle and the yarn back through the slip knot, forming a loop on the right-hand needle. Leave the slip knot on the left-hand needle.

3

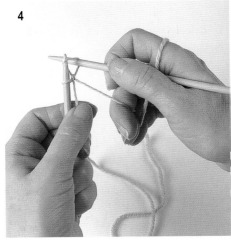

4. Transfer the new loop on to the left-hand needle. There are now two stitches on the left-hand needle.

4

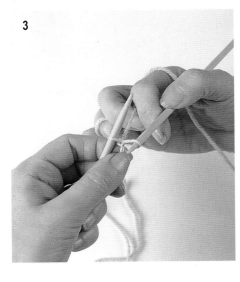

5. Insert the right-hand needle between the two stitches on the left-hand needle, and wind the yarn round the tip of the right-hand needle.

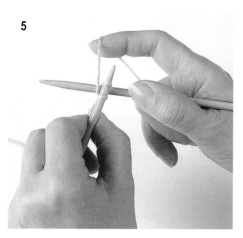

6. Draw a loop through again and place it on the left-hand needle.

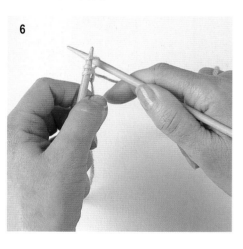

7. Repeat steps 5 and 6 until you have the required number of stitches.

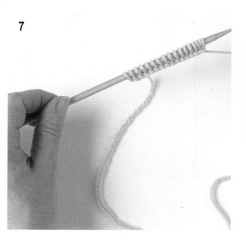

BASIC STITCHES
How to knit

The knit stitch is the most important stitch in knitting as it forms the basis for all knitted fabrics.

1. Hold the needle with the cast-on stitches in your left hand. With the yarn at the back, insert the right-hand needle from front to back through the first stitch on the left-hand needle.

2. Wind the yarn from left to right over the tip of the right-hand needle.

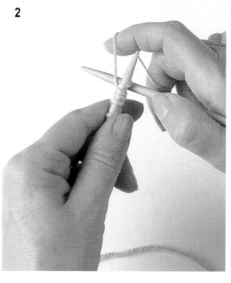

3. Draw the yarn through the stitch on the left-hand needle, making a new stitch on the right-hand needle.

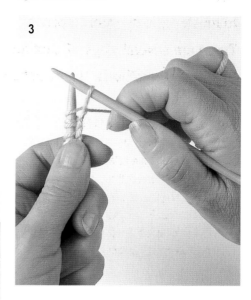

4. Slip the original stitch off the left-hand needle.

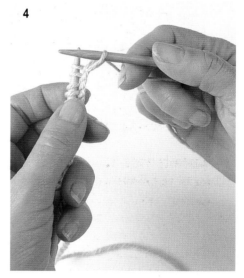

5. To knit a row, repeat steps 1 to 4 until all the stitches have been transferred from the left-hand needle to the right-hand needle. Turn the work and transfer the needle with the stitches on to the left hand to work the next row.

How to bind off

Binding off should be done in the same stitch and at the same gauge as the knitting — if it is too tight, the knitting will pucker. Try using a larger needle if you have problems.

1. Knit the first two stitches in the usual way, so both of the stitches are on the right-hand needle.

1

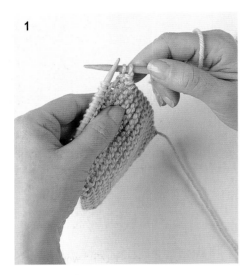

2. Use the tip of the left-hand needle to lift the first knitted stitch.

2

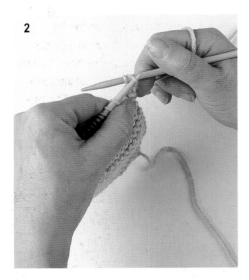

3. Pass this stitch over the second stitch and off the needle.

3

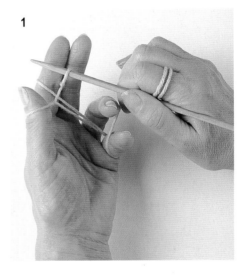

4. Knit another stitch on to the right-hand needle, and repeat from step 2 until one stitch remains. Lengthen the stitch and take it off the needle. Leaving a long length of yarn for seaming, pull the end of the yarn through the final stitch to tighten it.

4

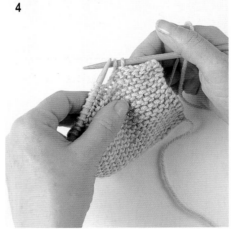

Left-handed knitters

Following the instructions for casting on, prop the book in front of a mirror and follow the diagrams in the mirror image. The yarn will then be controlled by the left hand.

Knitting by the Continental method may be the solution, because you are working in the same direction as a right-handed knitter, but holding the yarn in the left hand.

How to cast on – German thumb and finger method

This is a quick way of casting on using one needle. It is suitable for yarns with little elasticity, such as cottons.

Measure out approximately 1 inch of yarn for every stitch to be cast on. Make a slip knot at this point and slip it on the needle.

1. Wrap the ball end of the yarn around the left index finger and the cut end of the yarn around the left thumb. Wrap both ends of the yarn around the little finger.

1

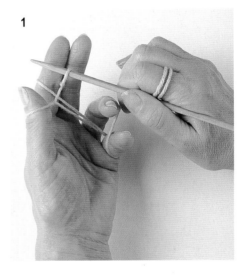

2. With the needle in the right hand, insert the tip of the needle upwards through the loop on the thumb and downwards through the loop on the index finger.

2

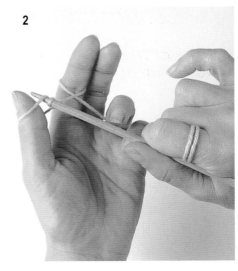

3. Draw the loop back through the loop on the thumb, then remove the thumb from the loop.

3

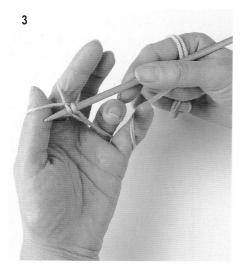

4. Use the thumb to pull the loop tight to form a new stitch.

4

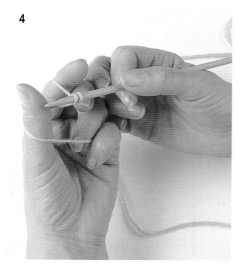

5. Repeat steps 1 through 4 until you have the required number of stitches on the needle.

How to knit – Continental style

This method of knitting is often used by left-handed knitters, because the yarn is controlled by the left hand.

1. Hold the yarn in your left hand with it looped round the index finger. Insert the right-hand needle from front to back into the stitch to be knitted, then twist it under the working strand of yarn from the index finger.

1

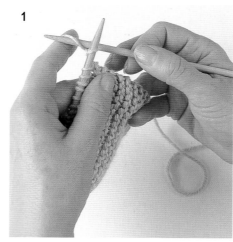

2. Use the right-hand needle to draw a new stitch through, then drop the loop from the left-hand needle.

2

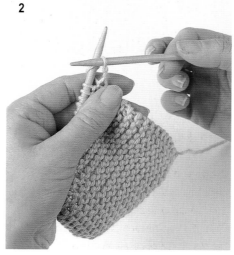

JOINING IN A NEW BALL OF YARN

Unless an enormous ball of yarn is used, it will be necessary at some time to join in a new ball of yarn.

1. Leaving enough yarn to darn in, and using a simple knot, join the new yarn to the long end remaining from the old ball.

1

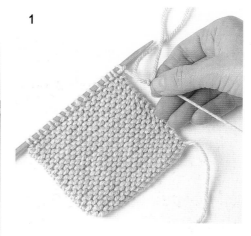

2. Slip this knot up close to the work before working the first stitch of the row.

SIMPLE SEAMS

Garter stitch lends itself to oversewing. The row ends form little loops that can be matched one for one and joined together. Thread the needle through the bottom of the stitch on one side and the top of the corresponding stitch on the other side. This produces a flat seam that does not interrupt the lines of garter stitch.

Following a Pattern

Most knitting patterns are produced by yarn manufacturers or appear in magazines or books. They give you all of the information you need to knit a garment that looks like the illustration. The information is usually presented in a logical form that is easy to follow.

MATERIALS

This is usually the first paragraph that appears on the pattern. It tells you how much yarn you need, what size needles to use, and whether you need cable needles or buttons, for example.

MEASUREMENTS

Measurements are very important. They tell you what the finished size of the garment will be. Compare the "actual measurements" with the "to fit" measurements; the amount of ease given may vary from style to style. You may want to adjust the size to fit you more comfortably. Once you have decided what size is for you, go through the pattern and mark it so that it is easy to read.

GAUGE

Gauge is the most important part of producing a perfect garment. The gauge that is stated in the pattern is the one obtained by the designer, using the quoted yarn and needle size. It is used to design the garment and produce the stated measurements.

MAKING AND MEASURING A GAUGE SWATCH

Always make a sample swatch, using the yarn and needles stated in the pattern. The gauge is usually given over 4 inches, but you should make a swatch that is at least 6 inches square. Place the sample on a padded surface and gently smooth it into shape without distorting the stitches. Pin the corners and sides as shown, below, unrolling the edges if necessary and inserting the pins at right angles to the fabric.

To find out the stitch gauge, use pins as markers and count the number of stitches

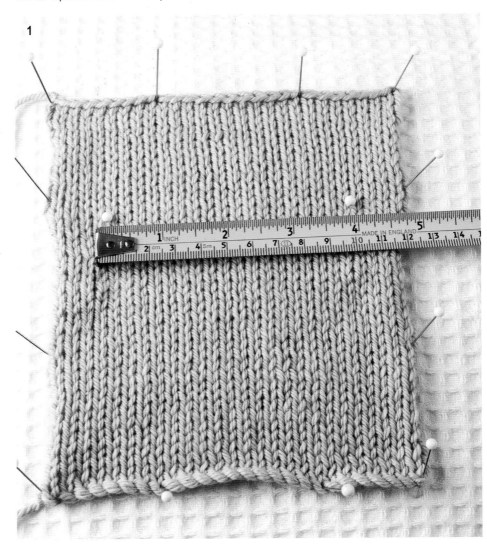

1

recommended in the gauge given in the instructions. Using a measuring tape, measure the distance between the pins. If your gauge is correct it should measure 4 inches. If there are less stitches than stated in the pattern, your knitting is too loose. If you have more stitches, your knitting is too tight. If your gauge is too loose make another swatch using smaller needles. If your gauge is too tight make another swatch using larger

needles. Your gauge must be accurate. If it is only one stitch off, it could make the finished garment too big or too small.

For the row gauge, follow the same procedure as for the stitch gauge. On stockinette stitch, it may be easier to work from the back as each ridge is one row. If your stitch gauge is accurate but your row gauge is slightly off, it should not make much difference to most garments.

ABBREVIATIONS

Abbreviations are used in knitting patterns to keep the instructions short and precise. If every word was spelled out, it would be like reading a book. The following abbreviations are the ones most commonly used:

alt	alternate
beg	beginning
cont	continue
dec	decreas(e)(ing)
folls	following
gst	garter st, every row k
inc	increas(e)(ing)
k	knit
m1	make 1 st by picking up the bar between the st just worked and the next st on the left-hand needle and working into the back of it
p	purl
patt	pattern
rem	remain(ing)
rep	repeat
RS	right side
sl	slip
skpo	slip 1, knit 1, pass slipped st over
st(s)	stitch(es)
st st	stockinette stitch, k on right side and p back
tbl	through back of loop
tog	together
WS	wrong side
yo	yarn over needle

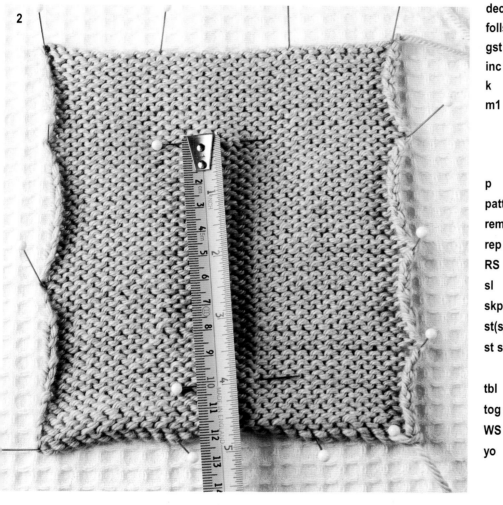

2

WRITTEN INSTRUCTIONS

Instructions are the main part of the pattern. They tell you how to make a garment from beginning to end. The instructions are given headings that are usually in a bold type so they are easy to spot . An asterisk (*) is a common symbol in knitting instructions. It is used to indicate that an instruction is repeated. For example, * p1, k1; rep from * to end

of row, means you just keep working p1, k1, until the last stitch has been knitted. Another space-saving technique is to put square brackets ([ ]) around instructions that are to be repeated and then state how many times they are to be repeated. For example, [p1, k1] 4 times.

Baby Hat and Scarf

Garter stitch produces a reversible fabric which makes it ideal for scarves and hats with fold up brims. To make this hat and scarf all you need to know is how to cast on, knit and bind off.

MEASUREMENTS

To fit age   0-3 months

MATERIALS

For the set
Debbie Bliss wool/cotton (1¾ oz. per ball): 3 balls in pale lilac or pale blue
Pair of size 5 knitting needles

GAUGE

25 stitches and 46 rows to 4 inches square measured over garter stitch using size 5 knitting needles.

SCARF

With size 5 needles, cast on 30 stitches.
Work in garter stitch (every row knit) until scarf measures 23½ inches from cast-on edge.
Bind off.

HAT

With size 5 needles, cast on 51 stitches. Continue in garter stitch (every row knit) until hat measures 14 inches from cast-on edge.
Bind off.

Finishing

Fold hat in half and join the two side seams. Fold brim to right side.

Basic Fabrics

All knitted fabrics are made using two basic stitches: knit and purl.

Garter stitch is often referred to as plain knitting because every row is knitted or purled. This produces a reversible fabric with raised horizontal ridges on both sides of the work. It is looser than stockinette stitch. One of the advantages of garter stitch is that it does not curl, so it can be used on its own or for bands and borders.

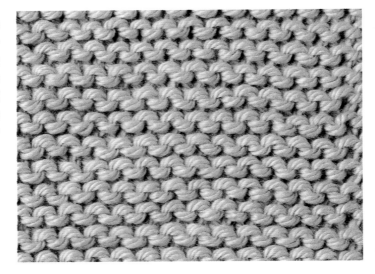

Stockinette stitch is the most widely used knitted fabric. With the knit side as the right side it makes a flat, smooth surface that tends to curl at the edges. It needs finishing with bands, borders, or hems where there would otherwise be a raw edge.

Reverse stockinette stitch is the "wrong side" of stockinette stitch and can be used in the same way as stockinette stitch. It is similar in appearance to garter stitch but gives a closer, flatter fabric.

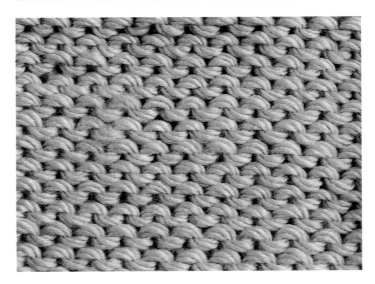

HOW TO PURL

Once you have mastered the art of knit stitch, the next step is learning how to purl.

1. Hold the needle with the stitches on in your left hand. With the yarn at the front of the work, insert the right-hand needle through the front of the first stitch on the left-hand needle.

1

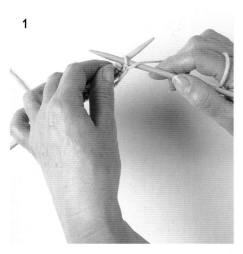

2. Wind the yarn from right to left over the tip of the right-hand needle.

2

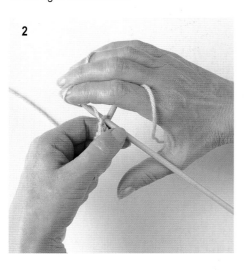

3. Draw the yarn through the stitch on the left-hand needle, making a new stitch on the right-hand needle.

3

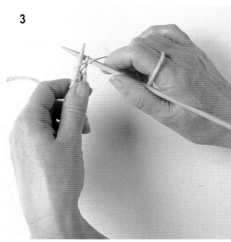

4. Slip the original stitch off the left-hand needle.

4

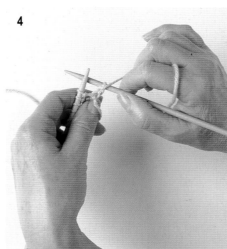

5. To purl a row, repeat steps 1 to 4 until all of the stitches have been transferred from the left-hand needle to the right-hand needle. Turn the work and transfer the needle with the stitches on to the left hand to work the next row.

How to purl — Continental style

1. Holding the yarn in your left hand and keeping your index finger to the right of where you are working, insert the right-hand needle from back to front through the stitch to be purled.

1

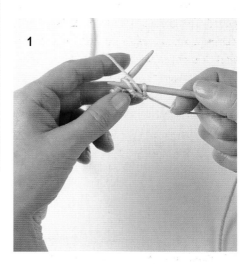

2. Bring the working yarn forward slightly, then twist the right-hand needle from left to right around the yarn. Draw a new stitch through and drop the original stitch from the left-hand needle.

2

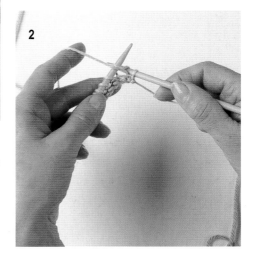

Three Easy Pillows

To make these charming pillows, all you need to know is how to cast on, knit, purl, and bind off.

GARTER STITCH CUSHION

MEASUREMENTS

12½ x 12½ inches.

MATERIALS

Jaeger Merino Aran (1¾ oz. per ball): 4 balls in dark grey
Pair of size 7 knitting needles
Pillow form, 14 x 14 inches

GAUGE

19 stitches and 25 rows to 4 inches square measured over garter stitch using size 7 needles.

Back

Cast on 61 stitches.
1st row: Knit to end.
This row forms the garter stitch pattern.
Continue in garter stitch until work measures 12½ inches from cast-on edge.
Bind off.

Front

Work exactly the same as for the Back.

Finishing

Sew the two cast-on edges together; then join the two pairs of side edges. Insert the pillow form, and join the remaining seam to finish.

STOCKINETTE STITCH CUSHION

MEASUREMENTS

13 x 13 inches.

MATERIALS

Jaeger Merino Aran (1¾ oz. per ball): 3 balls in cream
Pair of size 7 knitting needles
Pillow form, 14 x 14 inches

GAUGE

19 stitches and 25 rows to 4 inches square measured over stockinette stitch using size 7 needles.

Back

Cast on 63 stitches.
1st row: Knit to end.
2nd row: Purl to end.
These two rows form the stockinette stitch pattern.
Continue in stockinette stitch until work measures 13 inches from cast-on edge.
Bind off.

Front

Work exactly the same as for the Back.

Finishing

Sew the two cast-on edges together; then join the two pairs of side edges. Insert the pillow form, and join the remaining seam to finish.

STOCKINETTE AND GARTER STITCH CUSHION

MEASUREMENTS
12½ x 12½ inches.

MATERIALS
Jaeger Merino Aran (1¾ oz. per ball): 3 balls in grey
Pair of size 7 knitting needles
Pillow form, 14 x 14 inches

GAUGE
19 stitches and 25 rows to 4 inches square measured over stockinette stitch using size 7 needles.

Back
Cast on 61 stitches.
Knit 9 rows.
Next row: Knit to end.
Next row: Purl to end.
Repeat the last 2 rows three times more.
Knit 10 rows.
The last 18 rows form the pattern of stripes of stockinette stitch and garter stitch.
Continue in pattern until work measures 12½ inches from cast-on edge, ending with 10 rows garter stitch.
Bind off.

Front
Work exactly the same as for the Back.

Finishing
Sew the two cast-on edges together; then join the two pairs of side edges. Insert the pillow form, and join the remaining seam to finish.

Textured Stitches

Simple textured stitches are formed by working knit and purl stitches in the same row.

Moss stitch, also known as seed stitch, is a basic textured stitch. It is made up of alternating knit and purl stitches. Stitches that are knitted on one row, will be knitted on the next row and stitches that are purled on one row will be purled on the following row. If an odd number of stitches are cast on, every row will begin and end with a knit stitch. The fabric is firm, non-curling, and reversible, making it ideal for collars and cuffs.

For an odd number of stitches, the instructions will read:

Pattern row: Knit one stitch, * bring the yarn through the needles to the front of the work, purl the next stitch, take the yarn through the needles to the back of the work, knit the next stitch; repeat from * to end.

Repeat this row to form the pattern.

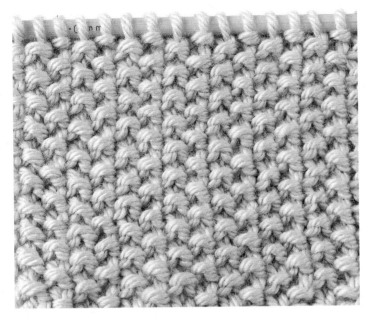

Single rib is formed by alternating knit and purl stitches to form columns of stitches. It produces a very elastic reversible fabric that is ideal for welts, neckbands, and borders. It is generally knitted on a smaller needle than the main fabric to keep it firm and elastic.

For an even number of stitches, the pattern will be as follows.

1. Knit the first stitch.

2. Bring the yarn through the needles to the front of the work and purl the next stitch (**A**).

3. Take the yarn through the needles to the back of the work and knit the next stitch (**B**).

4. Repeat steps 2 and 3 until all the stitches are on the right-hand needle, ending with a purl stitch.

5. Turn the work and start again from step 1.

A

B

Irish moss stitch is worked over four rows, the first two rows appear the same, then the stitches are alternated on the next two rows. This pattern is often used at the side of Aran stitches.

For an even number of stitches the pattern will be as follows.

1st row: * Knit 1 stitch, purl the next stitch; repeat from * to the end of the row.

2nd row: * Knit 1 stitch, purl the next stitch; repeat from * to the end of the row.

3rd row: * Purl 1 stitch, knit the next stitch; repeat from * to the end of the row.

4th row: * Purl 1 stitch, knit the next stitch; repeat from * to the end of the row.

Repeat rows 1 to 4 to form the pattern.

Double moss stitch is worked over a repeat of four stitches and four rows. It is usually worked over a multiple of four stitches with two extra stitches to balance the pattern.

1st row: Knit the first 2 stitches, * purl the next 2 stitches, knit the next 2 stitches; repeat from * to the end of the row.

2nd row: Purl the first 2 stitches, * knit the next 2 stitches, purl the next 2 stitches; repeat from * to the end of the row.

3rd row: Purl the first 2 stitches, * knit the next 2 stitches, purl the next 2 stitches; repeat from * to the end of the row.

4th row: Knit the first 2 stitches, * purl the next 2 stitches, knit the next 2 stitches; repeat from * to the end of the row.

Repeat rows 1 to 4 to form the pattern.

Double rib is worked over a repeat of four stitches and two rows. It is usually worked over a multiple of four stitches with two extra stitches to balance the pattern.

1st row: Knit the first 2 stitches, * purl the next 2 stitches, knit the next 2 stitches; repeat from * to the end of the row.

2nd row: Purl the first 2 stitches, * knit the next 2 stitches, purl next 2 stitches; repeat from * to the end of the row.

Repeat rows 1 and 2 to form the pattern.

Two Pretty Pillows and Basket-Weave Baby Blanket

Knit the two pillows to practice making knit and purl stitches in the same row. Once you are confident that you have mastered the techniques, try something slightly larger and knit a beautiful baby blanket.

BASKET-WEAVE PILLOW

MEASUREMENTS
12½ x 12½ inches.

GAUGE
19 stitches and 25 rows to 4 inches square measured over stockinette stitch using size 7 needles.

MATERIALS
Jaeger Merino Aran (1¾ oz. per ball):
4 balls in grey
Pair of size 7 knitting needles
Pillow form, 14 x 14 inches

once, then 6th row again.

These 10 rows form the pattern.

Continue in pattern until work measures 12½ inches from cast-on edge, ending with 10th row.

Bind off.

Front

Work exactly the same as for the Back.

Finishing

Sew the two cast-on edges together; then join the two pairs of side edges. Insert the pillow form, and join remaining seam to finish.

MOSS-STRIPE PILLOW

MEASUREMENTS

12½ x 12½ inches.

MATERIALS

Jaeger Merino Aran (1¾ oz. per ball):
4 balls in cream
Pair of size 7 knitting needles
Pillow form, 14 x14 inches

GAUGE

19 stitches and 25 rows to 4 inches square measured over stockinette stitch using size 7 needles.

Back

Cast on 61 stitches.

Begin with a knit row, work 8 rows stockinette stitch.

Moss stitch row: Knit 1, * purl 1, knit 1; repeat from * to end. This row forms the moss stitch pattern.

Work a further 7 rows in moss stitch.

These 16 rows form the pattern.

Continue working in pattern until work measures 12½ inches from cast-on edge, ending with 8 rows stockinette stitch.

Bind off.

Back

Cast on 60 stitches.

1st row: Knit 4, * purl 4, knit 4; repeat from * to end.

2nd row: Purl to end.

3rd to 5th rows: Repeat 1st and 2nd rows once, then 1st row again.

6th row: Knit 4, * purl 4, knit 4; repeat from * to end.

7th row: Knit to end.

8th to 10th rows: Repeat 6th and 7th rows

Front

Work exactly the same as for the Back.

Finishing

Sew the two cast-on edges together; then join the two pairs of side edges. Insert the pillow form, and join remaining seam to finish.

BASKET-WEAVE BABY BLANKET

MEASUREMENTS

Approximately 18½ x 23½ inches.

GAUGE

19 stitches and 32 rows to 4 inches measured over pattern using size 8 needles.

MATERIALS

Jaeger Merino Aran (1¾ oz. per ball):
5 balls in cream
Pair of size 8 knitting needles

Cast on 92 stitches.

1st row: Knit 4, * purl 4, knit 4; repeat from * to end.

2nd row: Purl to end.

3rd to 5th rows: Repeat 1st and 2nd rows once, then 1st row again.

6th row: Knit 4, * purl 4, knit 4; repeat from * to end.

7th row: Knit to end.

8th to 10th rows: Repeat 6th and 7th rows once, then 6th row again.

These 10 rows form the pattern.

Continue in pattern until blanket measures approximately 23½ inches from cast-on edge, ending with 10th row.

Bind off.

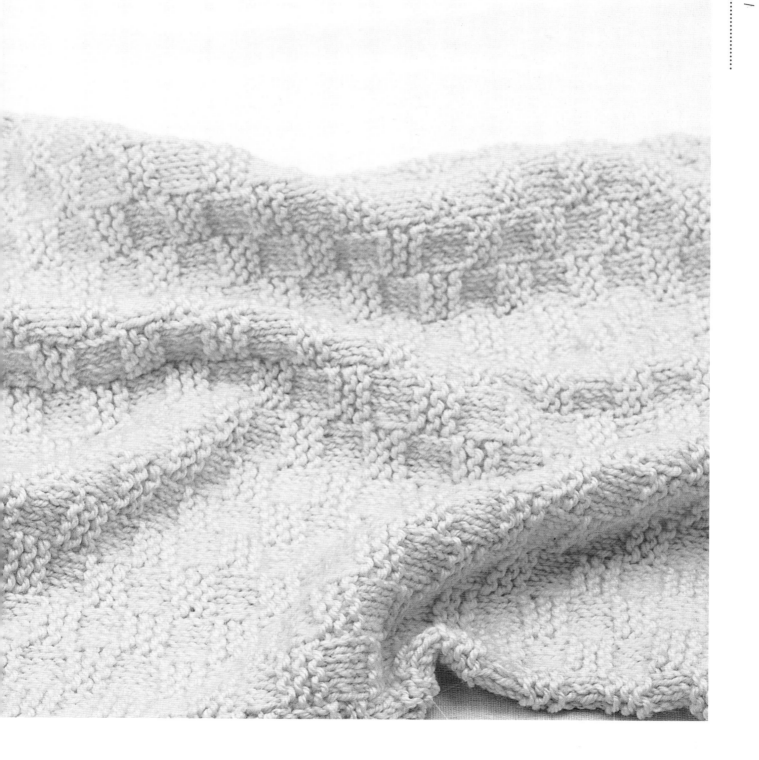

Simple Shaping

The easiest way to shape a garment is by working square corners. This doesn't involve any decreasing or increasing. If the garment is knitted in garter stitch, there's no need for extra edgings.

SHAPING A SQUARE NECK

1. Check the pattern to find out how many inches to work before you reach the neckline. The instructions will then tell you how to divide the stitches for each part of the neck. Work the number of stitches stated in the pattern, leaving the remaining stitches on a stitch holder or a length of yarn, ready to be worked later.

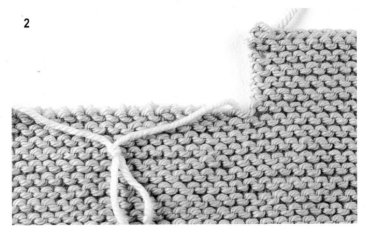

2. The instructions will now tell you what to do with the stitches on the needle to work the first side of the neck. Work straight until the knitting is the required length. Bind off.

3. Following the instructions, bind off the center stitches, then continue to work on the remaining stitches.

JOINING SHOULDERS

1. Lay the knitted pieces on a flat surface. Leaving a long end, secure a length of yarn to the first stitch, and insert the needle between the first and second stitches from the back of the work.

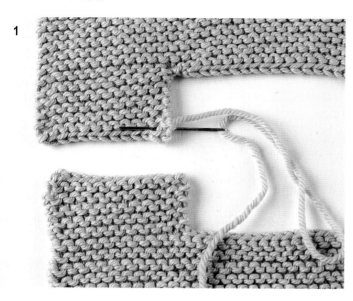

2. Take the needle across to the opposite piece, and from the back, insert between the first and second stitches.

3. Working backwards and forwards from one piece of knitting to the other, insert the needle from the front of the work into the space between the first and second stitch and bring it out in the space between the second and third stitch on the opposite piece.

4. Continue in this way for 2 inches; then pull the yarn up tight to join the seam close together. Continue in this way to the end of the seam.

5. Secure the ends by oversewing along the seam on the wrong side.

Garter-Stitch Pullover

Knit this darling sweater using the simplest of shaping methods.

MEASUREMENTS

To fit ages	6–12	12–18	18–24	24–36 months
Actual measurements				
Chest	20	22	24½	26½ inches
Length to shoulder	11	12¼	13½	15 inches
Sleeve length	6¼	7	8¼	9½ inches

MATERIALS

Debbie Bliss Merino double knitting (1¾ oz. per ball): 5 (5,6,7) balls in pale pink
Pair of size 6 knitting needles

Before making a
garment, it may be
useful to lay out the
pieces on a flat surface
so you can see how
they fit together.

Back

Sleeve

Sleeve

Front

GAUGE

22 stitches and 46 rows to 4 inches square measured over garter stitch using size 6 needles.

Back

With size 6 needles, cast on 56 (62,68,74) stitches.

Continue in garter stitch until back measures 10¼ (11½,12½,14¼) inches from cast-on edge, ending with a wrong side row.

Shape shoulders and back neck

Knit 16 (18,21,23) stitches, turn and work on this set of stitches only.

Continue straight until back measures 11 (12¼,13½,15) inches from cast-on edge, ending with a wrong side row.
Bind off.

With right side facing, rejoin yarn to next stitch, bind off center 24 (26,26,28) stitches, knit to end.

Continue straight on this group of 16 (18,21,23) stitches until back measures 11 (12¼,13½,15) inches from cast-on edge, ending with a wrong side row.
Bind off.

Front

Work as given for Back until front measures 9½ (10½,11¾,13½) inches from cast-on edge, ending with a wrong side row.

Shape shoulders and front neck

Knit 16 (18,21,23) stitches, turn and work on this set of stitches only.

Continue straight until back measures 11 (12½,13½,15) inches from cast-on edge, ending with a wrong side row.
Bind off.

NOTE
When working from instructions that pertain to more than one size, you may find it helpful to go through and highlight the figures for the size you are making.

With right side facing, rejoin yarn to next stitch, bind off center 24 (26,26,28) stitches, knit to end.

Continue straight on this group of 16 (18,21,23) stitches until back measures 11 (12¼,13½,15) inches from cast-on edge, ending with a wrong side row.
Bind off.

Sleeves

With size 6 needles, cast on 54 (56,58,60) stitches.

Continue in garter stitch until sleeve measures 6¼ (7,8¼,9½) inches.
Bind off.

Finishing

Join shoulder seams. Matching center of sleeve to shoulder seam, sew on sleeves using a back stitch. Join side and sleeve seams, leaving 1¼ (1¼,1½,1½) inches open at lower edge of side seams. Sleeves can be turned up to form a cuff.

Increasing

Increasing, by any one of a number of methods, is used to shape the fabric, making it wider.

KNITTING INTO THE SAME STITCH TWICE

1. On a knit row, knit first into the front of the stitch.

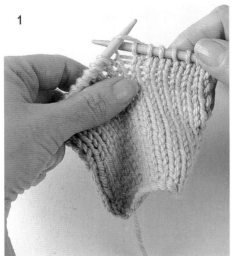

2. Then knit into the back of the same stitch, thus making two stitches from one.

PURLING INTO THE SAME STITCH TWICE

1. On a purl row, purl first into the front of the stitch.

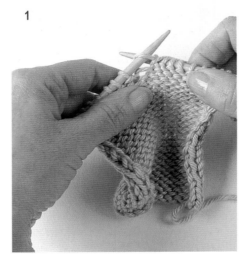

2. Then purl into the back of the same stitch, thus making two stitches from one.

INVISIBLE INCREASING

1. Before working the next stitch on the needle, knit into the stitch below the one on the needle.

2. Then knit into the next stitch on the needle. This method can also be used on a purl row.

RAISED INCREASING

1. Using the right-hand needle, pick up the bar that lies between the stitch just worked on the right-hand needle and the next stitch on the left-hand needle.

1

2. Place the bar on the left-hand needle, twisting it as you do, and knit into the back of it.

2

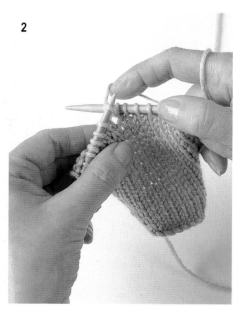

MAKING A STITCH BETWEEN TWO KNIT STITCHES*

Bring the the yarn to the front between the needles; then take it over the right-hand needle before knitting the next stitch.

MAKING A STITCH BETWEEN TWO PURL STITCHES*

Take the yarn over the right-hand needle to the back of the work; then bring the yarn to the front between the needles.

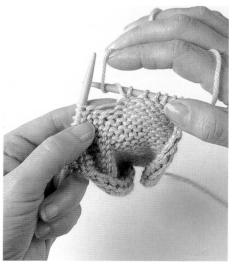

MAKING A STITCH BETWEEN A KNIT AND A PURL STITCH*

Having worked a knit stitch, bring the yarn forward under the right-hand needle; then wind it over the needle and back to the front. Purl the next stitch.

EXTENDING A ROW

Cast on the required number of stitches at the beginning or end of the row, using the usual method.

* Also called Yarn Over Increases, these stitches often create a little hole where made.

Child's Pullover with Moss Stitch Borders

Knit this pretty boatneck pullover with its moss stitch borders and shaped sleeves.

MEASUREMENTS

To fit ages	4-5	6-7	8-9	9-10 years
Actual measurements				
Chest	26¾	29¼	31½	33 inches
Length to shoulder	16½	17½	18½	19½ inches
Sleeve length	9½	10¼	11	11¾ inches

MATERIALS
Debbie Bliss wool/cotton (1¾ oz. per ball): 6 (7,8,9) balls in light sage green
Pair each size 2 and size 3 knitting needles

GAUGE
25 stitches and 34 rows to 4 inches square measured over stockinette stitch using size 3 needles.

Back

With size 2 needles, cast on 87 (95,103,109) stitches.

1st row: Knit 1, * purl 1, knit 1; rep from * to end.

This row forms the moss stitch pattern.

Repeat this row 7 times more.

Change to size 3 needles.

Beginning with a knit row, continue in stockinette stitch until Back measures 15¾ (16½,17¾,18½) inches from cast-on edge, ending with a purl row.

Change to size 2 needles.

Next row: Knit 1, * purl 1, knit 1; rep from * to end.

This row forms the moss stitch pattern.

Repeat this row 7 times more.

Bind off.

Front

Work exactly the same as for the Back.

Sleeves

With size 2 needles cast on 51 (53,57,59) stitches.

Work 8 rows in moss stitch as given for Back.

Change to size 3 needles.

Beginning with a knit row, continue in stockinette stitch as follows:

Work 4 rows.

Next row: Knit 2, make 1 stitch using the raised increase method, knit to last 2 stitches, make 1 stitch using the raised increase method, knit 2.

Beginning with a purl row, work 3 rows stockinette stitch.

Repeat the last 4 rows 16 (17,19,20) times more. 85 (89,97,101) stitches.

Work even in stockinette stitch until sleeve measures 9½ (10¼,11,11¾) inches from cast-on edge, ending with a purl row.

Bind off.

To Make Up

Join shoulder seams for 4 (4¼,4¾,5) inches. Sew on sleeves using a backstitch. Using the invisible seam method (see below), join side and sleeve seams, leaving the moss stitch borders at the lower edge of the side seams open.

Invisible seaming

This is the method most knitters use to obtain a professional finish. The seam is particularly suitable for straight stockinette stitch edges. You work from the front, so you can see exactly what you are doing.

1. With the right sides of both pieces of fabric facing upwards, join in the yarn, and thread the needle under the horizontal strand linking the edge stitch and the next stitch. Pass the needle under one row; then bring it to the front.

2. Return to the opposite side, and working under one row at a time throughout, repeat this zigzag action. Always take the needle under one row and insert it back into the hole that the last stitch on that side came out of. After you have worked 2 inches, pull the yarn up tight so that the work is pulled together creating a seam.

Decreasing

Decreasing, by any one of a number of methods,

is used to reduce the number of stitches, making

the fabric narrower

BASIC DECREASING

This is the simplest and most commonly
used method.

1. Insert the right-hand needle from left to
right through the second then the first stitch
on the left-hand needle.

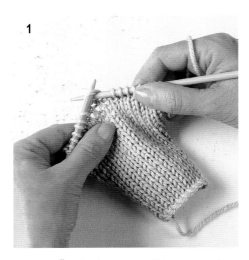

2. Knit the two stitches together, making one.

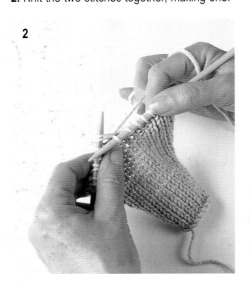

PURL DECREASING

1. Insert the right-hand needle from right to
left through the first two stitches on the left-
hand needle.

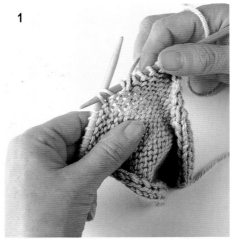

2. Purl the two stitches together, making one
stitch.

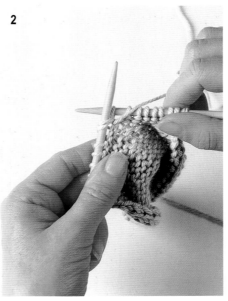

SLIP STITCH DECREASING

1. Slip a stitch from the left-hand needle on
to the right-hand needle. Knit the next stitch.

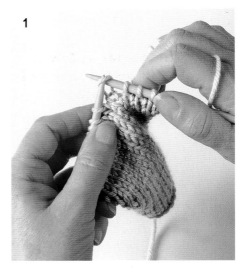

2. Then, using the tip of the left-hand needle,
pass the slipped stitch over the last stitch
on the right-hand needle and drop it off the
needle.

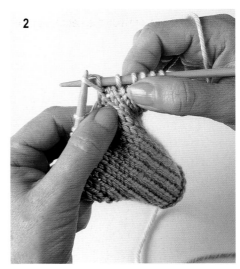

Basic Buttonholes

A buttonhole is a small closed slit worked in a border, used for fastening a button. It needs to be worked neatly or it will stretch and become non-functional. When following a pattern you will be told how many buttonholes to make and how far apart they should be.

EYELET BUTTONHOLES

These are the simplest buttonholes to make and are suitable for fine yarns and baby clothes.

Worked in garter stitch

1. Knit to the position of the buttonhole; then knit the next two stitches together.

1

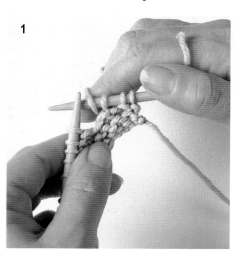

2. Bring the yarn between the needles to the front of the work.

2

Worked in rib

1. Work in rib to the position of the button-hole; bring the yarn between the needles; and take back over the right-hand needle.

1

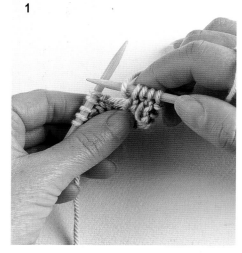

2. Either knit or purl the next two stitches together to keep the rib pattern correct.

2

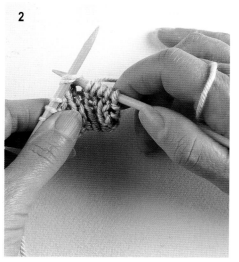

Worked in moss stitch

1. Work in moss stitch to the position of the buttonhole; bring the yarn between the needles; and take back over the right-hand needle. Work the next two stitches together to keep the pattern correct.

1

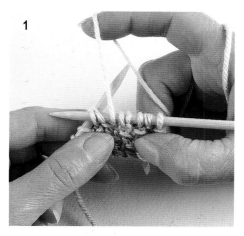

2. A small neat buttonhole is formed.

2

Cardigan with Garter-Stitch Stripes

With its simple shaping and buttonholes, this is ideal for your first "adult" project.

MEASUREMENTS

To fit	32	34	36 inches

Actual measurements

Bust	35¾	37¾	39¾ inches
Length to shoulder	21½	21½	21½ inches
Sleeve length	18	18	18 inches

MATERIALS
Jaeger Merino Double Knitting (1¾ oz. per ball):
10 (11,12) balls in cream
Pair each size 3 and size 6 knitting needles
6 buttons

GAUGE
22 stitches and 30 rows to 4 inches square
measured over stockinette stitch using
size 6 needles.

Back
With size 3 needles, cast on 102 (107,112)
stitches.
Knit 9 rows.
Change to size 6 needles.
Beginning with a knit row, work 8 rows in
stockinette stitch.
Knit 10 rows.
Repeat the last 18 rows 9 times more.
Bind off.

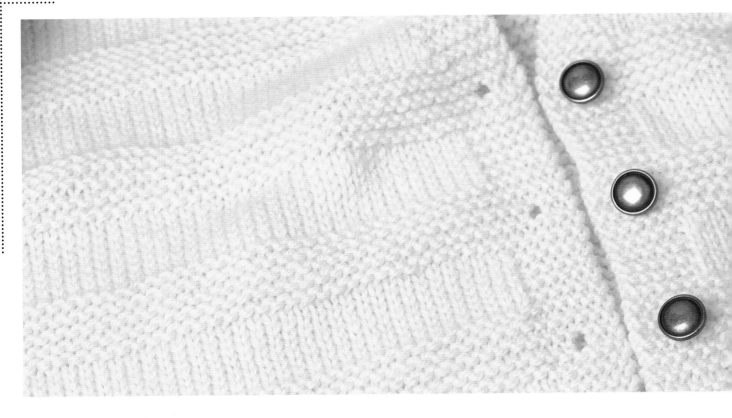

Left Front

With size 3 needles, cast on 54 (57,60) stitches.

Knit 9 rows.

Change to size 6 needles.

Work in pattern with 6 stitches in garter stitch at center front edge as follows:

1st row: Knit to end.

2nd row: Knit 6, purl to end.

Repeat the last 2 rows 3 times more.

Knit 10 rows.

Repeat the last 18 rows four times more.

Now work in pattern, shaping front edge for neck as follows:

1st row: Knit to last 7 stitches, knit 2 stitches together, knit 5.

2nd row: Knit 6, purl to end.

3rd row: Knit to end.

4th row: Knit 6, purl to end.

5th to 8th rows: Repeat 1st to 4th rows once more.

9th row: Knit to last 7 stitches, knit 2 stitches together, knit 5.

10th row: Knit to end.

11th row: Knit to end.

12th row: Knit to end.

13th row to 16th row: Repeat 9th to 12th rows once more.

17th row: Knit to end.

18th row: Knit to end.

Repeat the last 18 rows 3 times more. 38 (41,44) stitches.

Now work the 1st to 8th rows of neck shaping. 36 (39,42) stitches.

Knit 10 rows.

Now bind off for shoulder as follows:

Bind off first 30 (33,36) stitches; then knit remaining 6 stitches.

Continue in garter stitch on these stitches for a further 3½ inches for back neck border.

Bind off.

Right Front

With size 3 needles, cast on 54 (57,60) stitches.

Knit 3 rows.

Buttonhole row: Knit 2, knit 2 stitches together, bring the yarn to the front between the needles, then take over the right-hand needle, knit to end.

Knit 5 rows.

Change to size 6 needles.

Work in pattern with 6 stitches in garter stitch at center front edge as follows:

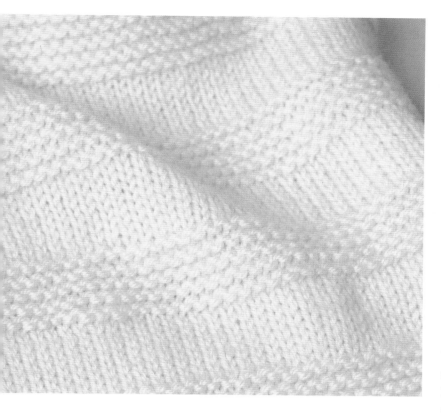

rows once more.

17th row: Knit to end.

18th row: Knit to end.

Repeat the last 18 rows 3 times more. 38 (41,44) stitches.

Now work the 1st to 8th rows of neck shaping. 36 (39,42) stitches.

Knit 10 rows.

Now bind off for shoulder as follows:

Knit 6 stitches, bind off remaining 30 (33,36) stitches.

With wrong side facing, join yarn to remaining 6 stitches.

Continue in garter stitch on these stitches for a further 3¼ inches for back neck border. Bind off.

Sleeves

With size 3 needles, cast on 46 (50,54) stitches.

Knit 9 rows.

Change to size 6 needles.

1st row: Knit 3, make 1 stitch using raised increasing method, knit to last 3 stitches, make 1 stitch using raised increasing method, knit 3.

2nd row: Purl to end.

3rd row: Knit to end.

4th row: Purl to end.

5th to 8th rows: Repeat 1st to 4th rows once more.

9th row: Knit 3, make 1 stitch using raised increasing method, knit to last 3 stitches, make 1 stitch using raised increasing method, knit 3.

10th to 13th rows: Knit to end.

14th to 18th rows: Repeat 9th to 13th rows once more.

Repeat the last 18 rows 6 times more. 102 (106,110) stitches.

Pattern a further 18 rows.

Bind off.

Finishing

Join shoulder seams. Join bound off edges of neck border. Sew neck border to back neck. With center of sleeve to shoulder seam, sew on sleeves, using a back stitch. Using the invisible seam method, join side and sleeve seams (see page 44). Sew on buttons.

1st row: Knit to end.

2nd row: Purl to last 6 stitches, knit 6.

Repeat the last 2 rows 3 times more.

Knit 4 rows.

Buttonhole row: Knit 2, knit 2 stitches together, bring the yarn to the front between the needles, then take over the right-hand needle, knit to end.

Knit 5 rows.

Repeat the last 18 rows 4 times more.

Now work in pattern, shaping front edge for neck as follows:

1st row: Knit 5, slip next stitch, knit next stitch, then pass the slipped stitch over the knitted stitch and off the needle, knit to end.

2nd row: Purl to last 6 sts, knit 6.

3rd row: Knit to end.

4th row: Purl to last 6 sts, knit 6.

5th to 8th rows: Repeat 1st to 4th rows once more.

9th row: Knit 5, slip next stitch, knit next stitch, then pass the slipped stitch over the knitted stitch and off the needle, knit to end.

10th row: Knit to end.

11th row: Knit to end.

12th row: Knit to end.

13th row to 16th row: Repeat 9th to 12th

Raglan-Sleeve Stockinette Stitch Sweater

So far, all of the instructions have been written out in full. The following instructions are given in full with the common abbreviations in bold.

MEASUREMENTS

To fit ages	2-3	3-4	4-5 years
Actual measurements			
Chest	28	31½	35½ inches
Length	13¾	15¾	17¾ inches
Sleeve length	8¾	10	11 inches

MATERIALS

Debbie Bliss Merino Aran (1¾ oz. per ball): 7 (7,8) balls in bright red
Pair each size 5 and size 7 needles

GAUGE

18 sts and 26 rows to 4 inches square measured over stockinette stitch **st st** using size 7 needles.

Back and Front (both alike)

With size 5 needles, cast on 66 (74,82) stitches **sts**.
Knit **K** 9 rows.
Change to size 7 needles.
Begin **Beg** with a knit **k** row, work in stockinette stitch **st st** until back measures 8 (8¾,9½) inches from cast-on edge, ending with a purl **p** row.

Shape raglan armhole

Bind off 5 (6,7) stitches **sts** at beginning **beg** of next 2 rows. 56 (62,68) stitches **sts**.
1st row: Knit **K** 3 stitches **sts**, slip **sl** 1 stitch, knit **k** 1 stitch, pass slipped stitch over **skpo**, knit **k** to last 5 stitches **sts**, knit 2 stitches together **k2 tog**, knit **k** 3.

2nd row: Purl **P** to end.
Rep the last 2 rows until 20 (22,24) **sts** rem, ending with a purl **p** row.
Change to size 5 needles.
Knit **K** 8 rows.
Bind off.

Sleeves

With size 5 needles, cast on 38 (42,46) stitches **sts**.
Knit **K** 9 rows.
Change to size 7 needles.
Beginning **Beg** with a knit **k** row, continue **cont** in stockinette stitch **st st**.
Work 4 rows.
Inc row: Knit **K** 3 stitches **sts**, pick up the bar between the stitch **st** just worked and the next stitch **st** on left hand needle and work into the back of it **m1**, knit **k** to last 3 stitches **sts**, pick up the bar between the stitch **st** just worked and the next stitch **st** on left hand needle and work into the back of it **m1**, knit **k** 3 stitches **sts**.
Beginning **Beg** with a purl **p** row, work 3 rows stockinette stitch **st st**.
Repeat **Rep** the last 4 rows until there are 60 (66,72) stitches **sts**.
Continue **Cont** even until sleeve measures 8¾ (10,11) inches from cast-on edge, ending with a wrong side **WS** row.

Raglan shapings may look difficult, but laid out flat it is easy to see how they go together. With fully fashioned shapings, the seams can be joined using the invisible seaming method.

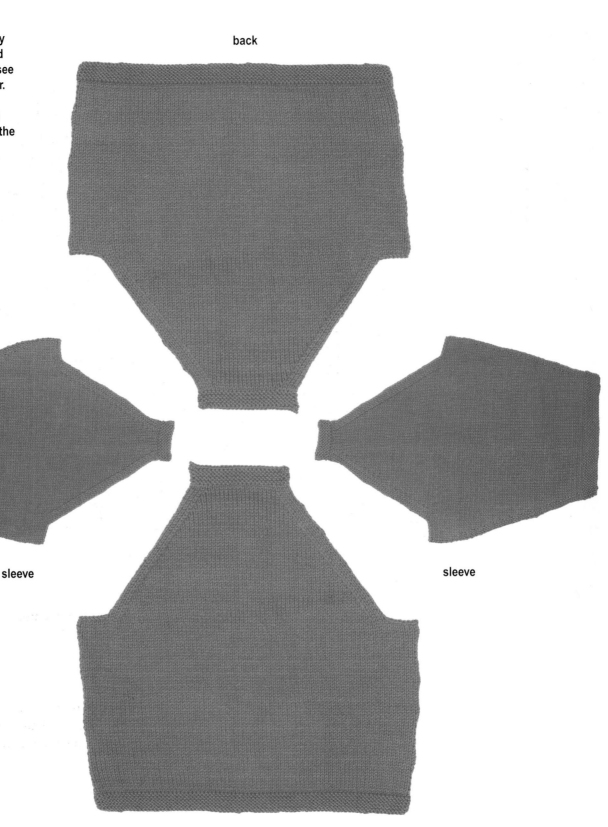

back

sleeve

sleeve

front

Shape raglan top

Bind off 5 (6,7) stitches **sts** at beg of next 2 rows. 50 (54,58) stitches **sts**.

1st row: Knit **K** 3 stitches **sts**, slip 1 stitch, knit 1 stitch, pass slipped stitch over **skpo**, knit **k** to last 5 stitches **sts**, knit 2 stitches together **k2 tog**, knit **k** 3.

2nd row: Purl **P** to end.

Repeat **Rep** the last 2 rows until 14 stitches **sts** remain rem, ending with a purl **p** row.

Change to size 5 needles.

Knit **K** 8 rows.

Bind off.

Finishing

Using the invisible seam method (page 44), join raglan and neckband seams. Join side and sleeve seams using the same method.

Working from a Chart

Working from a chart is usually associated with multiple color knitting, but simple textured motifs can also be worked from a chart.

MOTIF PATTERNS

These can either be written out in full, row by row, or drawn out in a chart form. The advantages of having a chart are that the motif is instantly visible and space is saved in the pattern instructions.

These can be worked in stockinette stitch on a reverse stockinette stitch background, reverse stockinette stitch on a stockinette stitch background, or moss stitch on either stockinette stitch or reverse stockinette stitch backgrounds.

The charts on these pages have a very simple key. A blank square indicates that a knit stitch should be used on a right-side row and a purl stitch on a wrong-side row. The second symbol indicates that a purl stitch should be used on a right-side row and a knit stitch on a wrong-side row.

ROWS

When reading the chart, odd numbered rows, which are numbered up the right-hand side of the chart, are right-side rows that are read from right to left; even numbered rows; which may be numbered up the left-hand side of the chart, are wrong-side rows that are read from left to right.

STITCHES

Usually only one repeat of the pattern is given in the chart; the stitches that form the repeat are usually indicated by the words "repeat these stitches." Any stitches that will not divide into the pattern are charted either side of the pattern repeat and are knitted at the beginning and ends of the rows to balance the pattern.

Start reading the chart from the bottom right-hand corner. The first square is the first stitch of the first row.

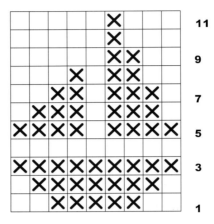

9 stitches

MORE MOTIFS.
These motifs can be used on their own, placing them at the center of the chest or in the corner of a garment. Something like the boat could be placed on the sleeve. The motifs could also be joined together to form a border.

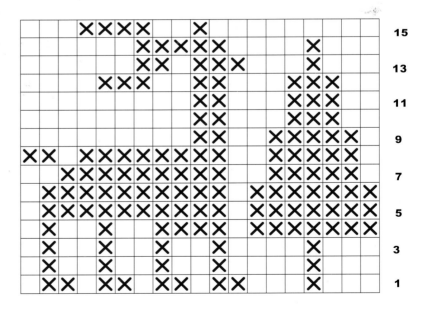

19 stitches

KEY

☐	k on right side and p on wrong side
☒	p on right side and k on wrong side

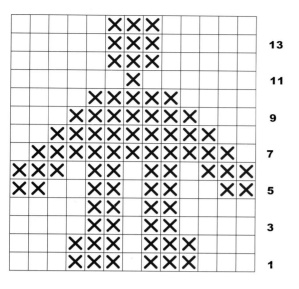

13 stitches

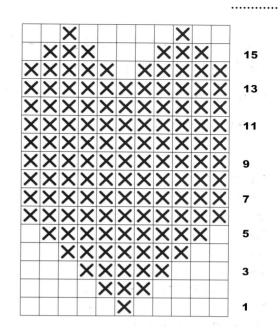

11 stitches

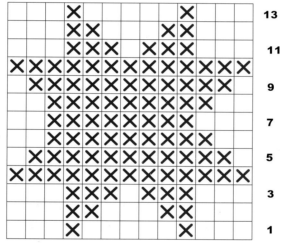

13 stitches

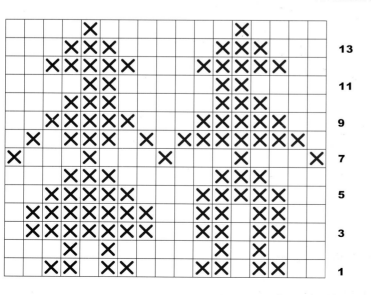

17 stitches

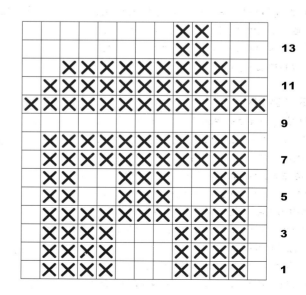

13 stitches

Picking up Stitches

Most edges of a knitted fabric will curl unless you knit a border after the garment is completed.

Once the main body of the knitting is compete, it is often necessary to pick up stitches to work a border; this might be a neckband, collar, front edging, cuffs, or armbands. The technique of picking up stitches along an edge is referred to as "pick up and knit," because stitches are made with new yarn rather than with the loops of the main fabric.

When working from a pattern, you will be told how many stitches to pick up. Be careful to pick up the stitches evenly along the edge, otherwise the fabric will buckle. A simple way to do this is to divide the edge into sections using pins. For instance, divide the edge evenly into eight sections. Then divide the number of stitches to be picked up by 8, and pick up this number of stitches in each section, checking the total number of stitches at the end.

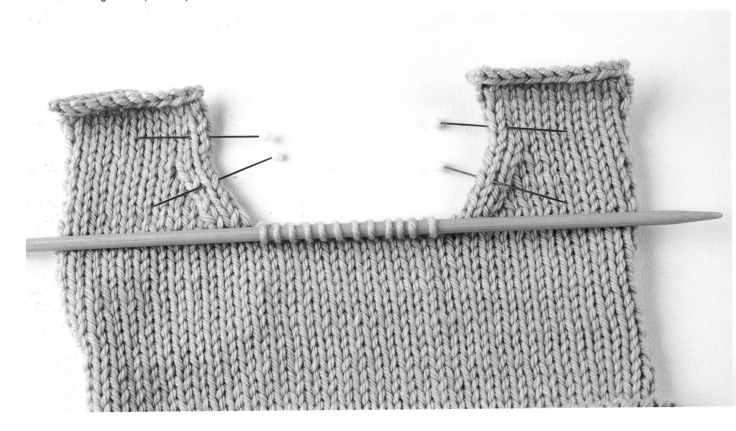

WORKING ALONG A CAST-ON OR BIND-OFF EDGE

1. With right side facing and holding a needle in your right hand, insert the point from front to back under both loops of the cast-on or bind-off edge. Wind the yarn around the needle as though knitting a stitch.

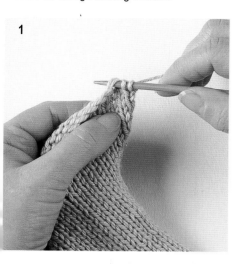

2. Draw a loop through, forming a stitch on the needle. Continue in this way until you have picked up the required number of stitches.

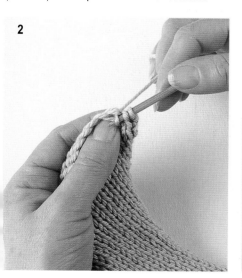

WORKING ALONG A SIDE EDGE

1. With right side facing and holding a needle in your right hand, insert the point from front to back between the first and second stitch in from the edge. Wind the yarn around the needle as though knitting a stitch.

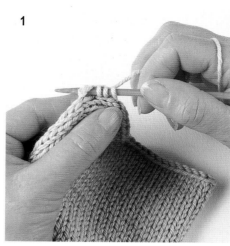

2. Draw a loop through, forming a stitch on the needle. Continue in this way until you have picked up the required number of stitches.

WORKING BORDERS

These are usually worked on a smaller needle than the main body of the garment.

1. A garter-stitch border is often worked along a front edge of a garment; this is especially suitable if you are going to insert a zipper.

2. Rib borders are most often used as an edging when a garment requires buttonholes.

Star-Motif Pullover

This simple cream sweater has a row of star motifs joined together to make a textured border.

MEASUREMENTS

To fit ages	1-2	2-3	3-4 years

Actual measurements

Chest	27½	30¼	33 inches

Length to shoulder

	14¼	15¾	17¾ inches

Sleeve length

	8¾	9½	10½ inches

MATERIALS

Rowan Wool/Cotton (1¾ oz. per ball): 6 (6,7) balls in cream
Pair each size 5 and size 6 knitting needles

GAUGE

22 sts and 30 rows to 4 inches square measured over st st using size 6 needles.

ABBREVIATIONS

beg	beginning
cont	continue
dec	decrease(ing)
folls	follows
inc	increase(ing)
k	knit
p	purl
patt	pattern
rem	remain(ing)
rep	repeat
st(s)	stitch(es)
st st	stockinette stitch, k on right side and p on wrong side

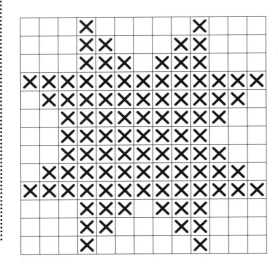

KEY

| | k on right side and p on wrong side |

| ☒ | p on right side and k on wrong side |

Back

With size 5 needles, cast on 78 (86,94) sts.

1st row: K2, * p2, k2; rep from * to end.

2nd row: P2, * k2, p2; rep from * to end.

Rep the last 2 rows 2 (2,3) times more.

Change to size 6 needles.

Dec row: K to end, dec one st at center. 77 (85,93) sts.

Next row: P to end.

Next row: K to end.

Next row: P to end.

Next row: P to end.

Next row: K to end.

Next row: K to end.

Next row: P to end.

Now work in patt as folls:

Next row: K4 (1,5) sts, now reading chart from right to left work across 1st row 5 (6,6) times, k3 (0,4) sts.

Next row: P3 (0,4) sts, now reading chart from left to right work across 2nd row 5 (6,6) times, p4 (1,5) sts.

Next row: K4 (1,5) sts, now reading chart from right to left work across 3rd row 5 (6,6) times, k3 (0,4) sts.

Next row: P3 (0,4) sts, now reading chart from left to right work across 4th row 5 (6,6) times, p4 (1,5) sts.

Cont in this way until all 13 rows have been worked.

Next row: P to end.

Next row: K to end.

Next row: K to end.

Next row: P to end.

Beg with a p row, cont in st st until back measures 14¼ (15¾,17¾) inches from cast-on edge, ending with a p row.

Shape shoulders

Bind off 25 (28,31) sts at beg of next 2 rows.

Leave rem 27 (29,31) sts on a spare needle.

Front

Work as given for Back until front measures 11¾ (13,14) inches from cast-on edge, ending with a p row.

Shape neck

Next row: K30 (33,36), turn and work on these sts for first side of neck.

Dec one st at neck edge on every row until 25 (28,31) sts rem.

Work even until front matches back to shoulder shaping, ending at side edge.

Shape shoulder

Bind off.

With right side facing, slip center 17 (19,21) sts onto a spare needle, rejoin yarn to rem sts, k to end.

Dec one st at neck edge on every row until 25 (28,31) sts rem.

Work even until front matches back to shoulder shaping, ending at side edge.

Shape shoulder

Bind off.

Sleeves

With size 5 needles cast on 50 (54,58) sts.

1st row: K2, * p2, k2; rep from * to end.

2nd row: P2, * k2, p2; rep from * to end.

Rep the last 2 rows 2 (2,3) times more.

Change to size 6 needles.

Beg with a k row, cont in st st, inc 1 st at each end of the 3rd and every foll 4th row until there are 74 (82,90) sts on the needle.

Now work even until the sleeve measures 8¾ (9½,10½) inches from cast-on edge,

ending with a p row.
Bind off.

Neckband

Join the right shoulder seam.

With size 5 needles, and right side facing, pick up and k15 (17,19) sts down left side of front neck, k across 17 (19,21) sts from front neck holder, pick up and k15 (17,19) sts up right side of front neck, k across 27 (29,31) sts from back neck holder. 74 (82,90) sts.

Next row: K2, * p2, k2; rep from * to end.
Next row: P2, * k2, p2; rep from * to end.
Rep the last 2 rows twice more.
Bind off in rib.

Finishing

Join left shoulder seam and neckband.
With center of sleeve to shoulder seam, sew on sleeves. Using the invisible seam method (page 44), join side and sleeve seams.

More Buttonholes

Garments made from bulky yarn and big buttons will require large buttonholes. Specific instructions will be given in the pattern.

VERTICAL BUTTONHOLES

These can be used for jackets made with thick yarn that requires big buttons.

1. Work to the position of the buttonhole. Join in another ball of yarn to the stitches on the left-hand needle.

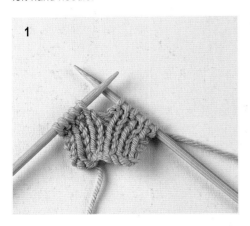

2. Continue to work each side separately with its own ball of yarn.

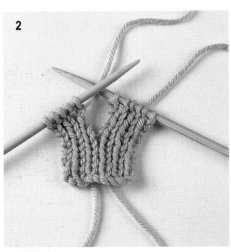

3. When the buttonhole is the required depth, close the gap by working across both sets of stitches with the first ball. Leaving a long end, cut off the second ball. To complete the buttonhole, use the ends from the second ball of yarn to strengthen the corners; then darn in the ends.

HORIZONTAL BUTTONHOLES

These are worked over two rows and used on cardigans and vests.

1. On a right-side row, work to the position of the start of the buttonhole. Working in pattern, bind off the required number of stitches; then work to the end of the row.

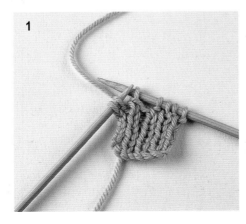

2. On the next row, work to the bind-off stitches. Turn the work, and cast on the same number of stitches using the cable method. Before placing the last cast-on stitch on to the left-hand needle, bring the yarn to the front between the stitches.

3. Turn the work, and complete the row.

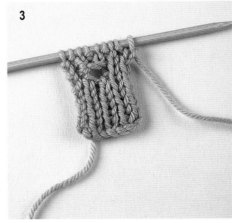

Working in Stripes

The simplest way of introducing a second color into knitting is to work in stripes. You can carry the yarn up the side of the knitting. This will save you from cutting off and joining in new balls of yarn every time you change color.

CREATING STRIPES

1. Using the second color, work a simple knot around the first color before starting to knit the row.

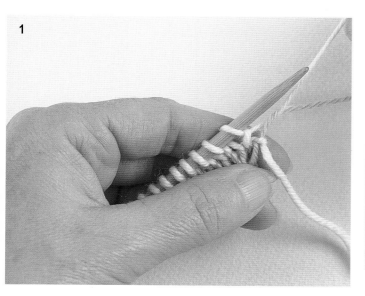

3. When the stripe is the required height, bring the first color around the second color so that it is ready for you to start knitting.

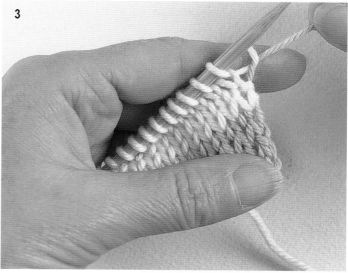

2. Before starting the next knit row, take the second color around the first color, "carrying" the first color up the side.

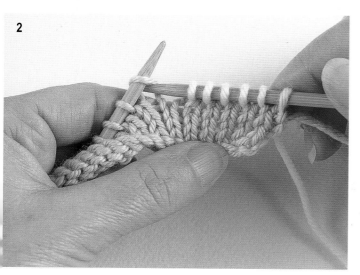

4. The "wrong" side of the fabric can also be used. The stripe is less defined and the effect is subtle.

Striped Pillows

These classic striped pillows, worked in stockinette stitch, look great in smart grays and creams, especially when piled up on a sofa with lots of other cushions

MEASUREMENTS

13 x 13 inches.

MATERIALS

Jaeger Merino Aran (1¾ oz. per ball):
4 balls (2 of each color)
Pillow form, 14 x 14 inches
Pair of size 7 knitting needles

GAUGE

19 stitches and 25 rows to 4 inches square over stockinette stitch using size 7 needles.

Back

Using first color, cast on 63 stitches.
1st row Using first color knit to end.
2nd row Using first color purl to end.
3rd row Using first color knit to end.

4th row Using first color purl to end.
Join in second color.
5th row Using second color knit to end.
6th row Using second color purl to end.
7th row Using second color knit to end.
8th row Using second color purl to end.
These eight rows form the stockinette stitch pattern and stripe sequence.
Continue in striped stockinette stitch until work measures 13 inches from cast-on edge, ending with 4 rows in one color.
Bind off.

Front

Work exactly the same as the Back.

Finishing

Sew two cast-on edges together; then join two pairs of side edges. Insert the pillow form, and join the remaining seam.

Striped Jacket

Use bold stripes to introduce cheerful color.

MEASUREMENTS

To fit ages	4-5	6-7	8-9	9-10 years
Actual measurements				
Chest	27	30	33	35 inches
Length to shoulder	15	16	17¼	18½ inches
Sleeve length	1¾	13	13¾	15 inches

MATERIALS

Debbie Bliss Merino Aran (1¾ oz. per ball): 4 (4,5,5) balls in navy and 4 (4,4,5) balls in cream
Pair each of size 7 and size 8 knitting needles
6 buttons

GAUGE

18 sts and 24 rows to 4 inches measured over st st using size 8 needles.

ABBREVIATIONS

beg	beginning
cont	continue
k	knit
m1	make 1 st by picking up the bar between the st just worked and the next st on left-hand needle and working into the back of it
p	purl
patt	pattern
rem	remain(ing)
rep	repeat
skpo	slip 1, knit 1, pass slipped st over
st(s)	stitch(es)
st st	stockinette stitch, k on right side and p back
tog	together
yo	yarn over needle

Back

With size 7 needles and Navy, cast on 64 (70,76,82) sts.

K 5 rows.

Change to size 8 needles.

Now work in stripe patt as follows:

Join in Cream.

Using Cream and beg with a k row, work 4 rows in st st.

Join in Navy.

Using Navy and beg with a k row work 4 rows in st st.

Cont in stripes of 4 rows Cream and 4 rows Navy until Back measures 15 (16,17¼,18½) inches from cast-on edge, ending with a wrong side row.

Shape shoulders

Bind off 21 (23,25,27) sts at the beg of the next 2 rows.

Change to size 7 needles.

Using Navy knit 6 rows.

Bind off.

Left front

With size 7 needles and Navy cast on 32 (35,38,41) sts.

K 5 rows.

Change to size 8 needles.

Now work in stripe patt as follows:

Join in Cream.

Using Cream and beg with a k row, work 4 rows in st st.

Join in Navy.

Using Navy and beg with a k row, work 4 rows in st st.

Cont in stripes of 4 rows Cream and 4 rows Navy until Front measures 10 (10¾,11½,12¼) inches from cast-on edge, ending with a wrong side row.

Mark beginning of last row with a colored thread. This denotes the beg of the neck shaping and will be useful when picking up stitches for the front band.

Shape front neck

Working in stripes, cont as follows:

Next row: K to the last 4 sts, k2 tog, k2.

Next row: P to end.

Repeat the last 2 rows until 21 (23,25,27) sts rem.

Now work even until the same number of rows have been worked as on the Back to shoulder, ending with a wrong side row.

Bind off.

Right Front

With size 7 needles and Navy cast on 32 (35,38,41) sts.

K 5 rows.

Change to size 8 needles.

Now work in stripe pattern as follows:

Join in Cream.

Using Cream and beg with a k row, work 4 rows in st st.

Join in Navy.

Using Navy and beg with a k row, work 4 rows in st st.

Cont in stripes of 4 rows Cream and 4 rows Navy until Front measures 10 (10¾,11½,12¼) inches from cast-on edge, ending with a wrong-side row.

Mark end of last row with a colored thread. This denotes the beg of the neck shaping and will be useful when picking up stitches for the front band.

Shape front neck

Working in stripes, cont as follows:

Next row: K2, skpo, k to end.

Next row: P to end.

Rep the last 2 rows until 21 (23,25,27) sts remain.

Now work even until the same number of rows have been worked as on the Back to shoulder, ending with a right side row.

Bind off.

Sleeves

With size 7 needles and Navy, cast on 32 (34,36,38) sts.

K 5 rows.

Change to size 8 needles.

Now work in stripe patt and shape sides as follows:

Join in Cream.

Using Cream and beg with a k row work 2 rows in st st.

Next row: K2, m1, k to last 2 sts, m1, k2.

P 1 row.

Join in Navy.

Using Navy and beg with a k row work 2 rows in st st.

Next row: K2, m1, k to last 2 sts, m1, k2.

P 1 row.

Rep the last 8 rows until there are 62 (68,74,80) sts on the needle.

Cont even until sleeve measures 11¾ (13,13¾,15) inches from cast-on edge, ending with a wrong side row.

Bind off.

Buttonhole band

Using size 7 needles and with right side facing and Navy, pick up and k50 (54,58,62) sts along right front edge to beg of neck shaping, then 32 (34,36,38) sts to shoulder. 82 (88,94,100) sts.

K 2 rows.

Buttonhole row: K37 (38,39,40) sts, [k2 tog, yo, k6 (7,8,9) sts] 5 times, k2 tog, yo, k3.

K 2 rows.

Bind off.

Button band

Using size 7 needles and with right side facing and Navy, pick up and k32 (34,36,38) sts along left front edge from shoulder to beginning of neck shaping, then 50 (54,58,62) sts to cast-on edge. 82 (88,94,100) sts.

K 5 rows.

Bind off.

Finishing

Join shoulder seams, carrying seam on through neck edgings. With center of sleeve to shoulder seam, sew on sleeves. Using the invisible seam method (page 44), join side and sleeve seams. Sew on buttons.

Pockets

Many garments feature pockets for both practical and decorative purposes. They fall into two categories – patch pockets, which are added afterwards, and pockets that are an integral part of the garment. Precise instructions are given with working patterns.

PATCH POCKETS

These pockets are added to the right side of a garment.

1. Mark where the pocket is to be positioned with contrast threads.

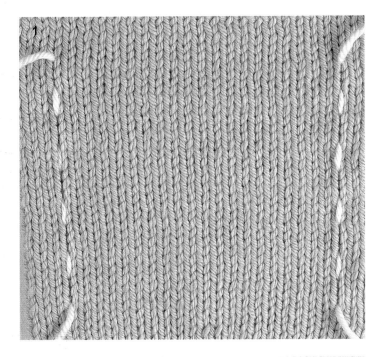

2. Pin the pocket in position on the background, lining the pockets up with rows and stitches. Using a slip stitch, sew the pockets in place.

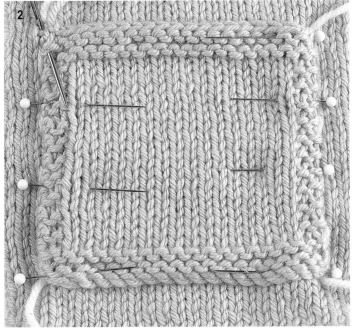

HORIZONTAL POCKETS

A horizontal pocket is knitted into the garment as an integral part of the design.

1. Make the lining in st st, ending with a p row. Cut off the yarn and slip the sts on to a holder. Work in pattern on the main part until you reach the pocket opening, ending on a wrong-side row. **Next row:** work to pocket position, and leave the group of stitches for the pocket on a length of yarn.

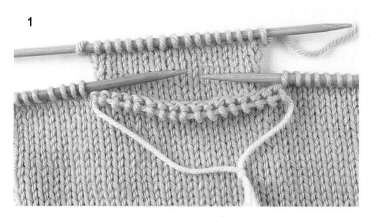

2. Work across the stitches of pocket lining, work to end of row.

3. When the garment is completed, the stitches on the length of yarn are worked in pattern to neaten the top. Sew down row ends.

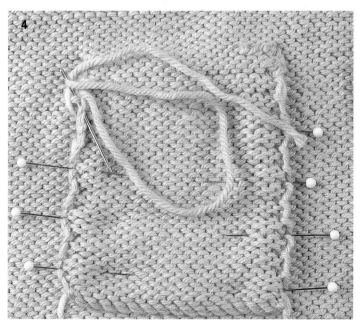

4. Pin the pocket lining in place on the wrong side and slip stitch in position.

Tunic with Pockets

Pockets are very easy to do when you follow these clear instructions.

MEASUREMENTS

To fit bust sizes	32	34	36 inches

Actual measurements

Bust	41	42½	44 inches

Length to shoulder	20½	21¼	22 inches

Sleeve length	18	18	19 inches

MATERIALS

Debbie Bliss Merino Aran (1¾ oz. per ball):
13 (14,15) balls in dark grey or claret
Pair each of size 7 and size 8 knitting needles

GAUGE

18 sts and 24 rows to 4 inches square over st st using size 8 needles.

ABBREVIATIONS

beg	beginning
cont	continue
dec	decrease(ing)
inc	increase(ing)
k	knit
m1	make 1 st by picking up the bar between the st just worked and the next st on left-hand needle and working into the back of it
p	purl
rem	remain(ing)
rep	repeat
st(s)	stitch(es)
st st	stockinette stitch, k on right side and p back

Back

With size 7 needles cast on 96 (100,104) sts.

K 7 rows.

Change to size 8 needles.

Beg with a k row, cont in st st until back measures 20½ (21¼,22) inches from cast-on edge, ending with a p row.

Shape shoulders

Bind off 33 (35,37) sts at beg of next 2 rows.

Leave rem 30 sts on a spare needle.

Pocket Linings (make 2)

With size 8 needles cast on 22 (24,26) sts.

Beg with a k row work 21 (23,25) rows in st st, ending with a k row.

Break yarn and leave sts on a holder.

Front

With size 7 needles cast on 96 (100,104) sts.

K 7 rows.

Change to size 8 needles.

Beg with a k row, work 18 (20,22) rows in st st, ending with a p row.

Place pocket

Next row: K13 sts, k next 22 (24,26) sts and leave these sts on a holder, k26 (28,30) sts, k next 22 (24,26) sts and leave these sts on a holder, k last 13 sts.

Next row: P13 sts, p across 22 (24,26) sts of one pocket lining, p26 (28,30), p across 22 (24,26) sts of second pocket lining, p13 sts.

Cont in st st until front measures 17¼ (18,19) inches from cast-on edge, ending with a p row.

Shape neck

Next row: K38 (40,42), turn and work on these sts for first side of neck shaping.

Dec one st at neck edge on every row until 33 (35,37) sts rem.

Cont even until front measures the same as back to shoulder, ending at side edge.

Shape shoulder

Bind off.

With right side facing, slip center 20 sts on to a holder, rejoin yarn to rem sts, k to end.

Complete to match first side.

Sleeves

With size 7 needles, cast on 36 (38,40) sts.

K 7 rows.

Change to size 8 needles.

Beg with a k row, cont in st st.

Work 4 rows.

Next row (inc row): K3, m1, k to last 3 sts, m1, k3.

Work 5 rows.

Rep the last 6 rows until there are 70 (74,78) sts.

Work even until sleeve measures 18 (18,19) inches from cast-on edge, ending with a p row.

Bind off.

Pocket tops

With size 7 needles, and right side facing, slip sts from pocket front on to a needle.

K 3 rows.

Bind off.

Neckband

Join right shoulder seam.

With size 7 needles, and right side facing, pick up and k15 sts down left side of front neck, k across 20 sts from front neck holder, pick up and k15 sts up right side of front neck, k across 30 sts from back neck holder. 80 sts.

K 13 rows.

Bind off.

Finishing

Join left shoulder and neckband seam. With center of sleeve to shoulder seam, sew on sleeves. Using the invisible seam method (page 44), join side and sleeve seams. Sew down pocket linings and pocket tops.

Resources

US

YARN AND OTHER SUPPLIES

Accordis Acrylic Fibers
15720 John J. Delaney Dr., Suite 204
Charlotte, NC 28277-2747
www.courtelle.com

Berroco, Inc
Elmdale Rd.
Uxbridge, MA 01569
(508) 278-2527

Boye Needle/Wrights
South St.
W. Warren, MA 01092
www.wrights.com

Brown Sheep Co., INC.
100662 County Rd. 16
Scottsbluff, NE 69361
(308) 635-2198

Cherry Tree Hill Yarn
52 Church St.
Barton, VT 05822
(802) 525-3311

Coats & Clark
Consumer Services
P.O. Box 12229
Greeneville, SC 29612-0224
(800) 648-1479
www.coatsandclark.com

Dale of Norway, Inc.
6W23390 Stonebridge Dr.,
Waukesha, WI 53186
(262) 544-1996

Elite Yarns
300 Jackson St.
Lowell, MA 01852
(978) 453-2837

Herrschners Inc.
2800 Hoover Rd.
Stevens Point, WI 54481
www.herrschners.com

JCA Inc.
35 Scales Lane
Townsend, MA 01469
(978) 597-3002

Lion Brand Yarn Co.
34 West 15th St.
New York, NY 10011
(212) 243-8995

Personal Threads
8025 West Dodge Rd.
Omaha, NE 68114
(800) 306-7733
www.personalthreads.com

Red Heart® Yarns
Two Lakepointe Plaza
4135 So. Stream Blvd.
Charlotte, NC 28217
www.coatsandclark.com

Rowan USA/Westminster Fibers, Inc.
4 Townsend West, Unit 8
Nashua, NH 03063
(603) 886-5041
www.knitrowan.com

Solutia/Acrilan® Fibers
320 Interstate N. Pkwy., Suite 500
Atlanta, GA 30339
www.thesmartyarns.com

TMA Yarns
206 W. 140th St.
Los Angeles, CA 90061

Trendsetter Yarns
16742 Stagg St.
Van Nuys, CA 91406
(818) 780-5497

Unique Kolours
23 North Bacton Hill Rd.
Malvern, PA 19355
(610) 280-7720

Yarns and ...
26440 Southfield Rd.
Lower Level #3
Lathrup Village, MI 48076-4551
(800) 520-YARN
www.yarns-and.com

ASSOCIATIONS

Association of Crafts & Creative Industries
1100-H Brandywine Blvd.
P.O. Box 3388
Zanesville, OH 43702-3388
(740) 452-4541

Craft Yarn Council of America
P.O. Box 9
Gastonia, NC 28053
Tel: 704-824-7838
www.craftyarncouncil.com

Crochet Guild of America
P.O. Box 127
Lockport, IL 60441
(877) 852-9190
www.crochet.org
www.cgoapresents.com

Hobby Industry Association
319 East 54th St.
Elmwood Park, NJ 07407
(201) 794-1133
www.hobby.org

The National Needlework Association
P.O. Box 3388
Zanesville, OH 43702-3388
(704) 455-6773
www.tnna.org

Society of Craft Designers
P.O. Box 3399
Zanesville, OH 43702-3388
(740) 452-4541

Western States Craft & Hobby Association
22033 Fries Ave.
Carson, CA 90745
(310) 549-5631

CANADA

Diamond Yarn of Canada Ltd.
155 Martin Ross Ave.
North York, ON M3J 2L9
(416) 736-6111
or
9697 St Laurent
Montréal, QC H3L 2N1
(514) 388-6188

S. R. Kertzer, Ltd.
105A Winges Rd.
Woodbridge, ON L4L 6C2
(800) 263-2354
www.kertzer.com

Koigu Wool Designs
RR1
Chatsworth, ON N0H 3H3
(519) 794-3066

Lily®
320 Livingston Ave. S.
Listowel, ON N4W 3H3
(519) 291-3780

Patons®
320 Livingstone Ave. S.
Listowel, ON N4W 3H3
www.patonsyarns.com

ASSOCIATIONS

Canada Craft & Hobby Association
#24 1410-40 Ave., NE
Calgary, AL T2E 6L1
(403) 291-0559

Canadian Crafts Federatopm
c/o Ontario Crafts Council
Designers Walk
170 Bedford Rd., Suite 300
Toronto, ON M5R 2K9
(416) 408-2294
www.canadiancraftsfederation.ca

Index

Acknowledgments

First and foremost, I would like to thank my mother who taught me to knit when I was five years old, so I could knit all the sleeves for my sisters' jumpers.

Thanks also to Rosemary Wilkinson, who invited me to write this book, Clare Sayer who patiently guided me through the all various stages of editing and book production, Shona Wood for her photography and lunches and Debbie Bliss, Jaeger Handknits and Rowan Yarns for their beautiful yarns. I must also thank the knitters: Dorothy Bayley, Cynthia Brent, Pat Church, Jacqui Dunt, Shirley Kennet, and Beryl Salter and Tricia McKenzie for checking all the patterns.

Finally, I'd like to thank my family, who didn't complain too much about the house being full of knitting yarn.